He

By Emily Schaubeck

For: Him

Emily Schaubeck

There will be days where I long for the
touch of your skin,
to feel the warmth of your smile,
and to see the stars in your eyes.

There will be nights where I will hear
your laughter echo,
through the walls of my heart,
and so I will wait for you
in that quiet moment.
I call it peace.

Emily Schaubeck

You have stars in your eyes
Like I have fire in my soul
And through the depths of my mind
You shine through the broken windows
of my heart

Emily Schaubeck

He walks towards me
With that funny little expression
On his face
The one where I cannot tell
Whether he is content
Or lost in a dream

Emily Schaubeck

You are the one who brings me back
to the world when I am lost in the
waters of self doubt

Emily Schaubeck

Simple is He
Who walked into my life
Not knowing of the adventures we would
share with the world

Emily Schaubeck

You are the poetry in me
The words that flow from my heart
Like waves

You are the music in my mind
And the one who will love me
Till the end of time

Emily Schaubeck

This guitar sings a sweet sadness
that can only be found in your voice.
The sound that runs through me,
like the shivers down my back

Emily Schaubeck

He is the one who knows me.
Like no other before
He went deeper into my soul,
and broke down the walls
I had built for myself

Emily Schaubeck

It is He who walks with me
Through the journey of life
Not before
And not after
But with me

Emily Schaubeck

Sweaters

You give me your sweaters
The ones that no longer fit you
But go down to my thighs
And I wear them with pride
To feel closer to you

And even when they are not
Too small
You give them to me anyways
Because it is a long and cold
train ride home
And you don't want me to get sick

I often wonder whether it is the
Protection I feel
Or your scent
that makes me feel warm inside

But at the end of the day
I know I am with you
No matter how far you may be
Whenever I wear your sweater

Emily Schaubeck

And even as I take this
Final train ride home
I can't help but think
To myself
How did I get so lucky?

Emily Schaubeck

I think back to the days
Where I listened to love songs
In the car with my mom...
I now understand what they mean

Emily Schaubeck

I've waited so long
For the right person
To fill my life with their presence.
I've broken hearts
And I've had my heart broken
But with you I see more.

Emily Schaubeck

Look out world
For here we come
Down the road
Hand in hand
With our minds at peace
And our hearts full

Emily Schaubeck

We Lost Our Hearts in Boston

We lost our hearts in Boston
When we took that road trip
To Massachusetts far from home.

When we found that amazing vegan restaurant and hiked
to the very top of a mountain
And when we sat on the bench In the park and we promised
to be faithful.

I gave you my heart
And I know you'll take good care of it
Through the rain and cold of
our hardships
But I will never forget Boston
And the days we spent
Just being

Emily Schaubeck

He is a work of art
A masterpiece
Crafted by the hands of the universe
And molded by time

He is a wonder
A gentle soul
That knows pain and suffering
But chooses to be kind
Always

Emily Schaubeck

His mind is free
Like a stallion over the plains
Or an eagle soaring through the open sky

Emily Schaubeck

From
Broken Birds

Emily Schaubeck

I wont ever try to fix you
I won't ever try to make you something you're not
And whilst you may be different from me
I will simply love you as you are

Emily Schaubeck

When the Rain Stops

I call out to you as the clouds roll in
To feel the sweetness in the air
Or the freedom in the wind

The power in the skies and the mellow in the breeze
My soul is at peace when I am with you
Or to hear your voice in the waves

A greater thing is felt when we are near
Like a ray of sun through the grey
Or the wholeness in my heart
When the rain stops

Emily Schaubeck

I watched the rays of sunlight
Shift through the trees
Of our open highway
In the woods
And I thought to myself
Things are good

Emily Schaubeck

Like day he came
And stole my heart
With the warmth of his presence
And with that his soul
And mine
Got lost in the calmness of the night

Emily Schaubeck

You gathered the scattered pieces
of my heart
You filled the emptiness
And made my life whole again

Emily Schaubeck

You shined your light
Into the darkness of my soul
And there I found peace
In the sound of your breath
Like the lullaby of the gentle
waves in the night

Emily Schaubeck

The Reason

You're the Reason I bloom in winter

You're the Reason I persevere when there is no hope

You're the Reason I stand on my own two feet when they knock me down

You're the Reason I come home

You are the Reason

Emily Schaubeck

With You

I long for the wind in my hair
Through the open fields of nowhere…
Like the long car rides we take for no reason
And the good
of feeling new

Emily Schaubeck

Pieces

You're a puzzle
Like the ones I see in toy stores
That are over five hundred pieces
And I know I'll never finish…
But I'll spend my time trying
Day in and Day out
Until all the broken pieces
Fit together with mine

Emily Schaubeck

Him

He sleeps quietly next to me
So I watch him
Breathing peacefully as he dreams
Things of wonder

He walks pleasantly next to me
So I watch him
Lost in thought with all the deep things
Of the world

He dances in the car next to me
So I watch him
Moving and singing along to the words
That help me understand him

I watch him almost everyday
As it is something I often do,
And yet I am still amazed
Every single time I see him

Emily Schaubeck

To He

Emily Schaubeck

You know I think of you
During the darkest hours of the night
And the brightest of days

Emily Schaubeck

The days without you will be rough
As I will be fooled
Every time I take the train

...

I will think I am going home to you

Emily Schaubeck

I am a dreamer
A lover
A fighter
A survivor

And all I am, I see in you

Emily Schaubeck

They throw around the word
Love
Like it is a little old thing found in a
Cardboard box of memories

They do not understand
It is much more than that

For
It is Us
And
It is We

Who give it life

Emily Schaubeck

It is a greater thing
We carry in our hearts
And keep with us always
When we doubt ourselves

Emily Schaubeck

There is no amount of
"I Love you"
That would be able to explain what
I feel for you.

And just like an over played song
They will forget about us
But what we feel for each other
Will always be

Emily Schaubeck

Give it Time

There are many who have given up
on Love
Because they feel it is not in the cards for them
Or maybe because they've tried
And had their heart broken

Every relationship
Friendship
Heart break
Must be a learning experience

Give it time
Because with it people grow

Nurture it

Emily Schaubeck

He is strong
He is valid
And when He is told to "man up"
And "Just deal with it"
He should not have to hide his feelings
from the world

Emily Schaubeck

I have made mistakes
And I will continue to make them
But through the days we've spent together
You've learned to accept me
For my flaws
For all I am
For what I stand for

Emily Schaubeck

Fear has dictated my life
From the day I entered this world

...

I have been a clockwork of
Intricacies and sorrows

...

But you have taught me to be
To expand the horizon of my mind

...

You have taught me to let go
Let go of the past

Emily Schaubeck

Wings

I look towards the sky
Watching the birds
And with that you took my hand
We spread our wings
And we flew

Emily Schaubeck

We are the ones who lead
We do not follow the crowd
And we do not run from
the overwhelming might of the enemy

Emily Schaubeck

Car Dancing

You shake your body to
the rhythms of the songs
we listen to in the car

Moving to the beats of
the sounds that can be heard
by every other car on the road

And it makes me feel whole
Seeing you
In that moment of bliss

Emily Schaubeck

There is beauty in the world
All around us
From every rock and tree
From every animal that roams
free
...
I found mine in you

Emily Schaubeck

Seeker

I used to seek fame and fortune
I used to seek a life of grandeur
And I used to hope and pray that
Maybe one day I might be someone
Worth something

I no longer seek greatness
I no longer seek power
I only seek enough success in life
To be comfortable

I seek a day where my heart is whole
My spirit is free
And things are good
Because you inspire me

Emily Schaubeck

He wrapped me up
Protected me from the world
Made me feel safe

He encouraged me to grow
To succeed
Because he believes in me

Emily Schaubeck

You rose above the crowd
With a smile that I could not resist
You changed my life in a way
I thought it would not
And my heart sang

Emily Schaubeck

I love you not for the sake of love
And not for the idea of being in love
But for the way we look into each others eyes
And the way we dance in the moonlight

Emily Schaubeck

So selfishly I begged for your love
When my heart was empty
And my mind was in the darkness,
Until I realized I didn't have to beg
I didn't have to beg
And I didn't have to wait
For you were always there
By my side
Holding my hand
Every step of the way

Emily Schaubeck

And as I sit here for an 8 1/2 hour bus ride
I realize that you are worth
Every second

Emily Schaubeck

We see the world through different eyes
And in many ways we are different
And the same
And although I may wander through a world
Of the unknown
I will always find my way home to
you

Emily Schaubeck

There are many words
And poems I could write
About you,
And the way you are
But none of it
Will ever come close to
My love for you

Emily Schaubeck

"We"

is a word I constantly find myself

using these days

...

Emily Schaubeck

And if you call my name
I will go to you
from wherever I am
No matter the distance
No matter of the circumstance
All you have to do is call

Emily Schaubeck

Where are the words?
The ones that I would use
to describe what we have,
there are none that would
do us justice.

Emily Schaubeck

Missing You

I'm missing you extra
today more than the rest,
because as I sit here and think about you
and what I should write
I cannot help but cry a little
because I am afraid

I am afraid of losing you
I am afraid of not being good enough
And I am afraid this distance will tear us apart

But I have faith
and I have hope
that things will be okay

So I'm sitting here missing you
But I'm wishing you the best
I'm wishing you happiness
And I hope you're having fun

- I love you

Emily Schaubeck

I feel the winds of loneliness
creeping through my bones
and making my skin shiver
But to reminisce of us
and to remember what
we have conquered
Is all I need
to know
it will
be
ok

Emily Schaubeck

The Breach

I've spent many days in the spotlight
and I've spent days wondering
wether I was good enough
but always in the cover of darkness
and always alone

But He reached through the darkness
He took my hand and taught me how to breathe

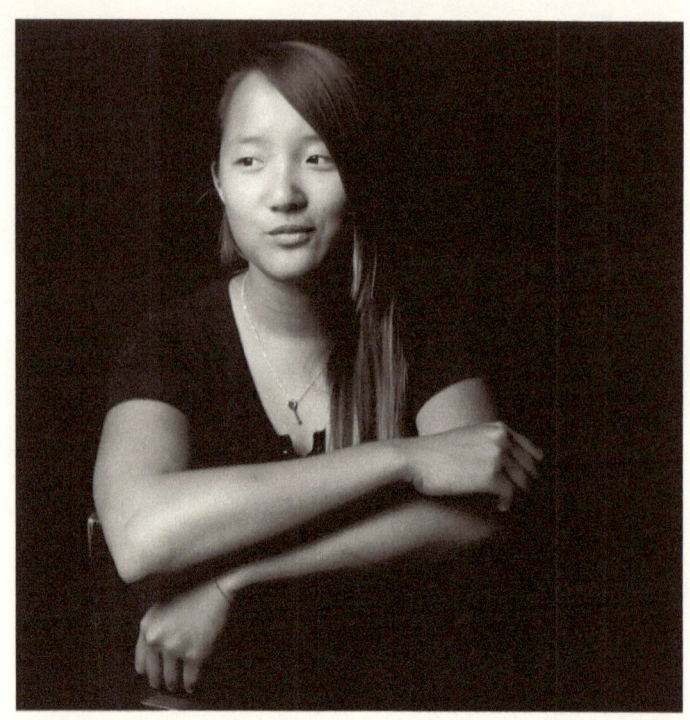

Emily Schaubeck

Follow Me

Instagram: @E.Schaubs
Facebook: Emily Schaubeck

Write Your Own:

www.ingramcontent.com/pod-product-compliance
Lightning Source LLC
Chambersburg PA
CBHW030506220526
45464CB00006B/2678